The Incredible FLOATING Dollar

Written by Gordon Hill
Illustrated by Heather Clarke
Photography by Stillview

tangerine press

Copyright © 2000 Scholastic Inc. Published by Tangerine Press™, an imprint of Scholastic Inc. 555 Broadway, New York, NY 10012. All rights reserved.

Scholastic and Tangerine Press™ and associated logos are trademarks of Scholastic Inc.

PUTTING ON A SHOW

This book tells you how to perform lots of magic tricks for your own magic show.

Before you show the tricks to anyone, you must practice them over and over again. Gather everything you need before you begin. Four of the tricks in this book use the special props from your Magic kit. Learn how the pieces work so that you can practice the tricks.

Many tricks need some secret preparation. Read each trick completely first, and try it out somewhere private. Keep on practicing until you can do it well. The best way to practice is to "perform" in front of a mirror, so you know exactly how the trick will look to your audience. When you are confident, you are ready to try out your trick on someone else.

You will find that the secrets revealed inside are really quite simple. That is true of almost all magic tricks. The most important part of magic isn't knowing HOW the tricks are done, it is the WAY that they are performed.

REMEMBER!
- Don't show a trick to an audience until you are really confident about performing it.
- Smile and chat throughout your performance and your audience will be drawn into each trick.
- Use magic words or your magic wand to add extra pizzazz to your show!

CLIPPED

This trick works by itself, so it's a nice easy one to start with. Use it to practice your performance skills!

Props box

- Paperclip
- Four Aces and any Queen
- Glue

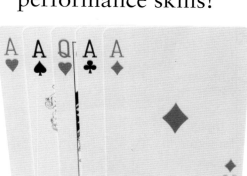

1 Prepare the trick by gluing the cards in a neat row with the Queen in the middle of the Aces.

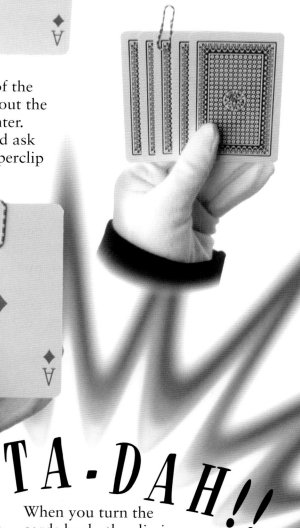

2 Show the faces of the cards and point out the Queen in the center. Turn the cards over and ask someone to put the paperclip on the center card.

TA·DAH!!

When you turn the cards back, the clip is nowhere near the center card!

THE INCREDIBLE FLOATING DOLLAR

Your audience will be amazed as you crumple up a dollar bill and make it float in midair!

Props box
- Magic thread (from your Magic kit)
- Dollar bill (from your Magic kit)
- Sticky tape

1 The secret of this trick is to practice, practice, and practice some more before you perform it in front of an audience. To prepare the trick, cut off about 4 feet (just over a meter) of Magic thread. Tease out a single fiber at one end, and gently pull it away from the other threads. When you have your single thread, don't lose it!

2 Tape the end of the thread in your performing area, about as high as your shoulder. Then fold a tiny piece of tape over the other end — this will go in your mouth to make the thread taut. The thread is invisible, especially against patterned backgrounds, but try not to work in a brightly lit area. Leave the loose end dangling for later.

3 Now for your performance. Show the dollar bill to your audience, so they can see that it has no wires attached, and no special tricks hidden within.

4 Take back the dollar, and at the same time pick up the end of your thread and pop it in your mouth. Disguise your action by scratching your face, or pretending to cough and covering your mouth. Tuck the tape between your cheek and gum (as if you're trying to hide chewing gum!).

5 Keep the thread taut as you lift the dollar to the thread, and slowly fold it in half around it, then crumple it up to keep it in place. Hold the bill with your left fingers and rest it on your right palm, then let go completely to leave it floating. Make sure it doesn't bounce on the thread!

TA-DAH!!

When the gasps have died down, move your hands around the note to "prove" that there is nothing holding it up. With practice, you can even learn to make the note move realistically, as if you are floating it from one hand to the other. To finish, unroll the note and pass it around for inspection again — secretly removing the thread from your mouth when no one is looking.

ROYAL TRAVELER

The King of Hearts from your hand seems to disappear and reappear at the other side of the room!

Props box

- Deck of cards
- Spare King of Hearts
- Scissors
- Glue

1 Prepare your trick by gluing a King of Hearts onto the face of an Ace of Spades and cutting the excess from the edges.

2 Hide your spare King of Hearts in the room, behind an ornament or on a bookshelf, to retrieve at the end of the trick.

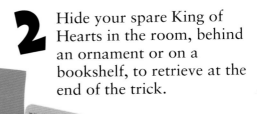

3 Hold two other Aces together and place them on top of the King, so it looks as if you are holding two Aces with a King in between. Show the fan of cards to your audience, face up.

4 Now turn the fan over, and at the same time spread the cards to separate the two Aces. Ask someone to take out the King.

5 They will remove the center card, which they saw was the King before you turned over the cards. When they turn it over, your whole audience will be shocked to see the card is an Ace.

TA·DAH!!

Now, direct someone to the real King in its hiding place. That's amazing!

DICEY FUTURE

Predict the roll of
the dice, even when
a volunteer shakes
them for you!

Props box

- Matchbox
- Four identical dice
- Pen and paper
- Envelope

1 Before your show,
glue two of the
dice into one end
of the matchbox drawer.
Place the drawer back in
the box.

2 On a piece of paper,
write down the total of
the two numbers that
show on the dice. Seal the
paper in an envelope.

3 Explain that you can make the dice
fall as you command. Ask someone
to place the other two dice into the
matchbox. Remember to open the empty
end of the box.

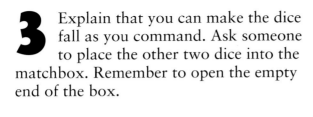

4 Ask her to shake the box, and even let her pass it to another member of the audience to be shaken some more.

5 Take back the box and open it up to show the glued dice. Ask your audience to add the two numbers on top of the dice.

TA·DAH!!

Have a member of your audience open the envelope. Everyone will be amazed at your powers of prediction!

MAGIC DISKS

Watch the black and white disks swap hands and back again — and then change color completely!

Props box
- Yellow/black disk
- Red/white piece
- Blue/white disk
- Green/black piece
(all from your Magic kit)

1 Away from your audience, stick the red piece face down on the yellow disk so that the disk is black and white. Stick the green piece face down on the blue disk so that's black and white, too.

2 Now show your audience your outstretched hands, with a black disk in one hand and a white in the other.

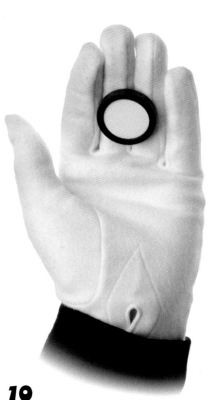

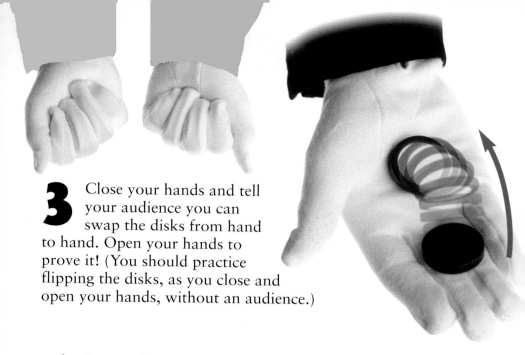

3 Close your hands and tell your audience you can swap the disks from hand to hand. Open your hands to prove it! (You should practice flipping the disks, as you close and open your hands, without an audience.)

4 Repeat the same movements to amaze your audience again. Now, just when they may think they have got you figured out, show them the disks have changed color completely! Simply swap the disks from hand to hand, and touch the two black sides together. This will transfer the loose piece and reveal the colors underneath.

5 Finally, swap hands again, this time touching the two white sides together. Yet again, your audience will be amazed to see two more colors!

INTERNATIONAL MAGIC

Identify the very
coin that was
chosen while your
back was turned...

Props box

- A few foreign coins, all different
- Paper bag

1 Put all the coins in the
bag and ask someone to
pick out one coin,
without letting you see it.

2 Turn your back and
ask him to pass the
coin around so that
everyone can have a good
look. Turn around to let
him drop the coin back in
the bag.

TA-DAH!!

Reach inside the bag and
pull out his chosen coin. This
should be easy, as it will be
warmer than all the others
after being handled so much!

THE MAGNIFICENT 7

Your prediction comes true — your volunteer really does choose the seven pile!

Props box

- Deck of cards
- Pen and paper
- Envelope

1 Before your audience arrives, write "You will choose the seven pile" on your paper and seal it in the envelope.

2 For your audience, deal three piles of cards, face down. What no one knows is that the piles have been arranged beforehand: the first is the four Sevens, the second is a Four, a Two and an Ace (adding up to seven), and the last pile contains any seven cards.

TA·DAH!!

Now ask a volunteer to choose any pile and turn it over. When the envelope is opened, your prediction is correct!

MONEY ON THE MOVE

Move a coin from underneath a glass — without touching it!

Props box

- Two large coins
- One smaller coin
- Glass
- Handkerchief
- Tablecloth

1 Put the two large coins on a table (which must have a tablecloth on it), a little bit apart. Put the small coin between them and cover it with the glass, so the rim is resting on the two outer coins.

2 Cover the glass with the handkerchief. Explain that you are going to get the coin out from underneath the glass without touching anything. Wave your wand over the glass and concentrate all of your magical powers on the coin.

3 What your audience doesn't know is that you are secretly scratching the tablecloth behind the glass with your other hand. Use the first finger of one hand, but distract the audience's attention with your wand-waving and magic words.

TA·DAH!!

When you remove the handkerchief, the coin is outside the glass! You will have to practice this beforehand to see how long it takes for the coin to move from underneath the glass as you scratch.

BUNGLING BURGLARS

As you tell the tale of the four bungling burglars raiding your deck of cards, all four are caught making their getaway!

Props box

• Deck of cards

1 Show the four Jacks in a fan. Don't let your audience see that there are three other cards (any cards) hidden behind the first Jack. Tuck them away tightly.

2 Close the fan and put it on top of the deck, explaining that the Jacks are burglars and the deck is the building.

3 Tell your tale of the burglars roaming the building to do their wicked business. Each burglar is moved to a different floor by removing the top card each time and placing it elsewhere in the deck as you talk. Move the top card to the "lower floors" and the next two burglars to "higher floors". Put the fourth burglar on the bottom as a lookout.

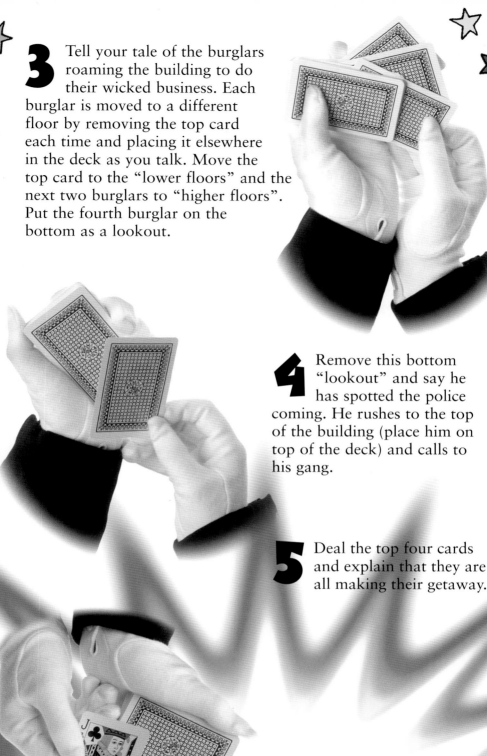

4 Remove this bottom "lookout" and say he has spotted the police coming. He rushes to the top of the building (place him on top of the deck) and calls to his gang.

5 Deal the top four cards and explain that they are all making their getaway.

TA-DAH!!

Turn over the four cards you have dealt. Surprise, surprise, they are the four Jacks!

SOFT COINS

Not one, not two, but THREE coins from your audience are soft enough to push pencils through!

Props box

- Coin case (from your Magic kit)
- Three pencils
- Three coins
- Piece of paper

1 Before you start, press the plastic pointer into the hinge of the case to release the sliding tray. Now, show the case to your audience, tipping it forward so the tray stays inside the case.

2 Ask for coins to be placed in each of the three holes. Place the paper over them and close the case. The paper should be cut to size, about 7 in. x 2 in. (18 cm x 5 cm).

3 Tip the case towards you and the tray should slide out, hidden by the paper.

4 Poke each of the pencils through the holes, starting at the end. Your audience will be amazed! If you hold the case carefully, concealing the tray, you can even turn the case over to show your audience both sides.

5 To finish the trick, remove the pencils and tip the case away from you to slide the coins back into position. Lock it back in place by pushing the small bump sticking out from the hinge end (the end pointing away from you).

TA·DAH!!

Take away the paper and return the coins to their owner — pointing out that the coins aren't damaged, but the paper is proof that the pencils were pushed right through!

A CUT ABOVE THE REST

How can you cut a piece of string in two but leave it in one piece? That's magic!

Props box

- Piece of paper, about 8 in. x 6 in. (20 cm x 15 cm)
- String, about 16 in. (40 cm)
- Scissors

1 Fold the paper as you see in the picture. Lay the string across the paper so your audience can see it.

2 Now lift the paper and tip the string into the bottom fold. What your audience cannot see is that your thumb stops the center of the string from falling down.

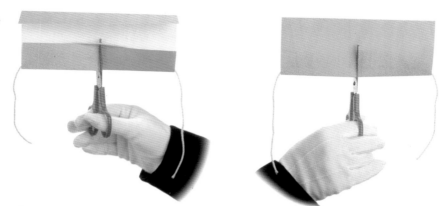

3 Cut right through the paper from bottom to top, making sure that the scissors go behind the center part of the string (the part held back by your thumb).

4 Keep the two halves together so everyone thinks the string has been cut into two. Now, crumple up the paper and say you will restore the string to one piece.

TA·DAH!!

Pull it out of the paper as a whole string!

COIN VANISHER

Make a coin — or any small object — vanish into thin air before your audience's eyes!

Props box
- Coin
- Small rubber band
- Handkerchief

1 Secretly place a small rubber band over the thumb and first two fingers of your left hand.

2 Lay the handkerchief over your hand and open your fingers underneath, stretching the band. Show a coin and push it into the center of the handkerchief, so you can hold it with the fingers of your left hand. Say your magic words, then grab one corner of the handkerchief, and shake it in the air.

TA-DAH!!

It appears that the coin has vanished, but really it is hidden in a secret pocket in the handkerchief made by the rubber band.